Drawing as Therapy

The School of Life

Published in 2021 by The School of Life
First published in the USA in 2021
70 Marchmont Street, London WC1N 1AB

Copyright © The School of Life 2021

Designed and typeset by Marcia Mihotich

Printed in Lithuania by Balto Print

A proportion of this book has appeared online at
www.theschooloflife.com/thebookoflife

Every effort has been made to contact the copyright
holders of the material reproduced in this book. If any
have been inadvertently overlooked, the publisher will be
pleased to make restitution at the earliest opportunity.

The School of Life is a resource for helping us understand
ourselves, for improving our relationships, our careers
and our social lives – as well as for helping us find calm
and get more out of our leisure hours. We do this through
creating films, workshops, books and gifts.

www.theschooloflife.com

ISBN 978-1-912891-59-7

10 9 8 7 6 5 4 3 2 1

FSC
www.fsc.org

MIX
Paper from
responsible sources
FSC® C107574

Contents

Introduction

This is a drawing book for people who can't draw. It won't help you get any better at drawing. It won't teach you how to sketch an outline, shade an object, use proper perspective or correct proportions. There are no hints on how to produce limbs like Leonardo or torsos like Titian. All it aims to do is to encourage you to draw – or, perhaps more accurately, to encourage you to draw *again*...

Why We Stop Drawing

To begin with, all of us draw. From the moment humans are first able to close a fist around a crayon or pencil, we start to scribble, sketch, etch and colour. We draw stick figures and lop-sided houses, fluffy clouds and smiling suns. We draw on pads, chalkboards, crepe paper – perhaps even (problematically) on the walls. Our early efforts probably didn't show any particular talent, but they may still have been praised and treasured by our parents and caregivers (unless the living room wall was our canvas).

Then, all of a sudden, around adolescence, most of us stop. From time to time, we might pick up the habit again – an absent-minded doodle on the back of an envelope during a boring phone call, or a simple sketch of a dinosaur to amuse a child – but for all intents and purposes, our drawing life is over.

Why does something that once came to us so naturally, an act as instinctive as breathing, become so inaccessible? In most cases, this is an unfortunate by-product of art education.

The act of drawing is conceived differently for adults than it is for children. When practised by a child, drawing is seen as a piece of playful, creative self-expression; a way for a small person to convey their distinctive personal perspective on the world. It helps them process their experiences and explore their characters and emotions.

Yet, in the adult world, this conception of the purpose of drawing is largely abandoned. Instead, as we are taught by teachers and instructors, drawing becomes seen primarily as a skill or discipline whose main purpose is to render objective reality as accurately as possible. We learn that there are rules – of scale, perspective, weight and shadow – that must be revered and followed. We learn that our work will be assessed and criticised on the basis of its quality. Unless we prove adept at mastering such rules (or are willing to persevere despite any skills), it's likely that many of us will stop drawing altogether.

This book rejects this view of the purpose of drawing. It seeks to rehabilitate drawing as a valid act of self-expression for adults as well as children.

Furthermore, it suggests a further conception, one that has nothing to do with skill at all. Far from being a simple practice or discipline, it holds that drawing can be a form of therapy.

Art is Therapy

One of the first people to notice that drawing might have therapeutic benefits was the British artist Adrian Hill (1895–1977). During the First World War, Hill was employed as a sketch artist for a company of scouts, sent over the top to quickly sketch the layout of enemy trenches. In the late 1930s, he contracted tuberculosis and spent several years recovering in a sanatorium. While confined to his bed, he began to sketch objects he could see in his room – vases, lampshades, doctors, medical instruments – and became convinced that doing so helped to speed up his recovery. When the Second World War broke out, he chose to stay on at the sanatorium to run art classes for wounded soldiers. It was around this time that he first coined the term 'art therapy'. His experiences and ideas were detailed in his 1945 book *Art Versus Illness*.

Another British artist who was inspired by Hill's approach was Edward Adamson (1911–1996), who volunteered to help with Hill's programme after the war. Adamson's great insight was that art therapy could be useful in helping people recover not only from physical trauma (like illness or injury) but also psychological trauma.

In 1946, he began to teach Hill's methods at Netherne mental hospital in Surrey, England, where he would remain for the next 35 years. In that time, he created a vast complex of studios and galleries in the buildings and grounds and amassed more than 60,000 works of art from his patients, which he displayed in regular public exhibitions.

At the core of Adamson's teaching was a 'non-interventionist' approach to art. Unlike at a traditional art school, his students were never instructed on how or what to draw; they were merely encouraged to draw what they felt like. Moreover, their artwork was never analysed for its possible meanings by anyone other than the artist themselves. What they drew didn't matter – it was the act of drawing itself that was important.

Two artworks by Mary Bishop, a patient at Netherne and a student of Adamson's for more than 30 years. Her many paintings were displayed in the hospital gallery to help the doctors and nurses empathise with the ways her fellow patients might be thinking and feeling.

Adamson saw this act as a form of 'self-recovery', whereby aspects of one's mind and personality that have been hidden or suppressed through trauma can emerge again through art. In so doing, they can be accessed and re-integrated into the patient's self and psyche, thereby helping them recover from the trauma and return to a state of inner cohesion.

Today, art therapy is a large and diverse movement, taught by many different practitioners and dedicated associations across the world. While there are numerous competing theories as to its exact purpose and benefits, this book largely follows Adamson's manifestly simple approach: that the act of drawing, coupled with a self-reflective mindset on the part of the artist, offers an opportunity for healing.

How to Use This Book

This book contains 80 drawing exercises. None of them demand a level of skill, and a number encourage us to abandon notions of quality altogether.

The purpose of the exercises is self-knowledge. They are an invitation for us to reflect on different aspects of our lives and minds by attempting to render these in visible form. Although the book makes suggestions about what we should draw, the tone is never prescriptive. Readers are free to interpret the exercises however they wish.

We don't have to be in a state of mental distress to benefit from the exercises. They aim to benefit everyone, at all times, but may be especially fruitful in difficult stretches.

The exercises are divided into eight sections. Each section corresponds to a particular area of life, a deeper understanding of which is fundamental to attaining a fulfilled mindset. We can work through them in any order we wish, and complete as many of the exercises as we feel will be beneficial.

Most importantly, with therapeutic art, there is no such thing as failure or success: only self-discovery and, in the best sense, play.

1 Play

First and foremost, for children at least, drawing is a form of play – a spontaneous, imaginative act that amuses and delights. Children's ignorance of traditional rules is indulged by adults because we recognise, if only dimly, that play is a valuable part of their growth. It is precisely at the point that drawing ceases to be seen as play (and becomes instead another form of work) that most of us drop the habit.

This book holds a different view: that play is a valuable, meaningful and therapeutic act at any age. An early proponent of this view was the paediatrician and psychologist Donald Winnicott (1896–1971). Winnicott recognised the vital role of play in the psychological and emotional development of adults as well as children. In his 1971 book *Playing and Reality*, he wrote, "it is in playing and only in playing that the individual child or adult is able to be creative and to use the whole personality, and it is only in being creative that the individual discovers the self."

Winnicott is the inventor of the 'squiggle game' – an activity he developed for parents to play with their child, which we have included in this section.

In the following exercises, you'll be discovering yourself through the act of spontaneous, unconscious creativity – what Winnicott called 'desultory formless functioning'. Here especially, we want you to abandon any thought as to the quality of your work; it should only feel enjoyable, irreverent and fun.

Donald Winnicott's Squiggle Game

Turn the squiggles on this page into drawings, incorporating the squiggle into the design. Think about what the shape of the squiggle suggests to you. Might one of them look like a mouth? The brim of a hat? An elephant's trunk? Try to go with your very first spontaneous impression.

Draw Like a Child

Near the end of his life, observing children's artwork on a tour of a primary school, Pablo Picasso remarked, "It took me four years to paint like Raphael, but a lifetime to paint like a child."

On this page, you are encouraged to draw like a child. You are allowed to:
* Use a crayon, felt tip or coloured pencil.
* Ignore any notion of scale and perspective.
* Colour outside the lines.
* Be ruled only by the limits of your imagination.

Drawing in the Dark

Turn off all the lights. Spend two to five minutes drawing in complete darkness.
Attempt a portrait from memory, or simply draw whatever comes to mind.

Turn on the lights. See what your mind's eye has produced.

Badly Drawn Horses

The British artist L. S. Lowry (1887–1976), renowned for his landscapes of industrial Manchester in the north of England, famously couldn't paint horses. When required to include one in a picture, he would strategically position it behind walls or carts to avoid having to paint the whole animal.

Draw a horse as badly as you can – one L. S. Lowry might have been proud to be ashamed of.

Object Subject

Giuseppe Arcimboldo (1526–1593) became famous for his portraits of subjects composed entirely of objects: flowers, berries, gourds, vegetables and toads. The chosen objects would in some way symbolise the sitter – a librarian assembled from books, for example. Arcimboldo was revered by later surrealists for the subversive weirdness of his vision.

Draw a self-portrait in the manner of Arcimboldo: one composed entirely of objects. Choose those that in some way speak to or symbolise your personality – for example, pencils if you enjoy writing or piano keys if your passion is music.

Imaginary Cartography

Draw a map of an imaginary country – a place you might wish to visit, live or, were you a monarch, to rule over. Plot the coasts, rivers, roads, terrains, vegetation, habitations and landmarks. Give it a name. Feel free to be fanciful and to blend the geographical and the emotional. There might be a Lake of Tenderness and a Cave of Comfort, for example.

Out of Proportion

Typically, drawing instructors will try to teach us how to draw figures with 'correct' proportions; that is, how to accurately capture the scale of various parts of the human body. Perhaps the most famous drawing in existence – Leonardo da Vinci's *Vitruvian Man* – is an exercise in rendering precise proportions. Our own early efforts probably didn't follow these rules, but what they lacked in accuracy, they gained in distinctiveness and character.

Draw a series of figures with wildly incorrect proportions. They might have elongated arms and a tiny head; humongous ears and a minuscule nose; a pigeon chest and elephantine feet...

One Liner

Paradoxical as it might seem, a crucial element of play is the embrace of restrictions. Creativity flourishes not through total freedom (which can be paralysing), but under the imposition of constraints.

See if you can sketch something in your immediate vicinity – an object in the room, say, or the outline of your own hand – without ever separating your pen from the paper: creating a portrait composed of a single, unbroken line. If you make a mistake, don't give up – simply try to incorporate it into the drawing as best you can.

Comic Strip

Use the empty panel comic strips provided. Choose a recent incident or anecdote from your own life (preferably one with a good punchline) and depict it in comic story form.

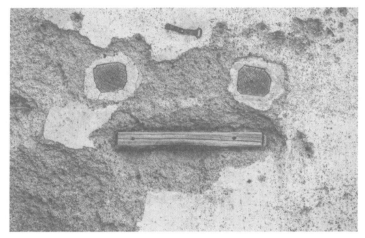

Pareidolia

'Pareidolia' refers to our tendency to recognise faces in inanimate objects such as clouds, car bonnets, electrical sockets and other everyday items.

See if you can draw some examples. Look around your house and try to spot any faces you find. Are they grinning or frowning? Excited or scared? Draw them.

2   Self

Artists and art lovers alike have always been fascinated by self-portraits. They are the purest embodiment of the notion that art is ultimately a reflection of the artist, offering a window into their psyche or soul. Some of the most famous and revered artists, from Rembrandt to Frida Kahlo, are today most celebrated for their unflinching paintings of themselves.

For the artist, it isn't just the availability of a free and willing subject (though this is a benefit) that makes the form appealing. Rather, a self-portrait can be a highly therapeutic form of self-discovery. Rembrandt wrote that "Life etches itself onto our faces... showing our violence, excesses or kindnesses."

The act of self-portraiture allows us to step outside ourselves so that we might see our identities more clearly. We become our own subject, seen for the mixed-up, flawed, pitiable yet loveable creatures we really are.

In the following exercises, you'll be invited to create a series of self-portraits. These won't be traditional self-portraits. Instead, you'll be asked to draw several internal aspects or dimensions of your self, perhaps ones that are buried or hard to consider day to day. You'll be looking at yourself from emotional angles and perhaps spotting a new logic or coherence.

Self-Portraits

Find four or more photographs of yourself at different ages in your life, from infancy, to youth, to maturity, to the present day. Draw self-portraits from these photographs on this page, capturing the breadth of your experience in a single picture. Note that none of these portraits is the true 'you'– instead, your self is the sum of each of them.

My Best and Worst Feature

Draw what you've always considered to be your best feature. It might be a realistic rendering of a physical attribute (your eyes, or the shape of your ears) or an abstract representation of a characteristic of your personality (loyalty, generosity). Try to capture what you value about this part of yourself.

Next, draw your worst feature. Again, this might be realistic (an unfortunate nose, a stooping posture) or abstract (cowardice, vanity).

If I Were an Animal...

Draw yourself as if you were an animal. Choose the creature that seems to best embody your inner self. If no one animal seems to capture the core of your personality, draw a chimera (a mythical creature made up from parts of other animals).

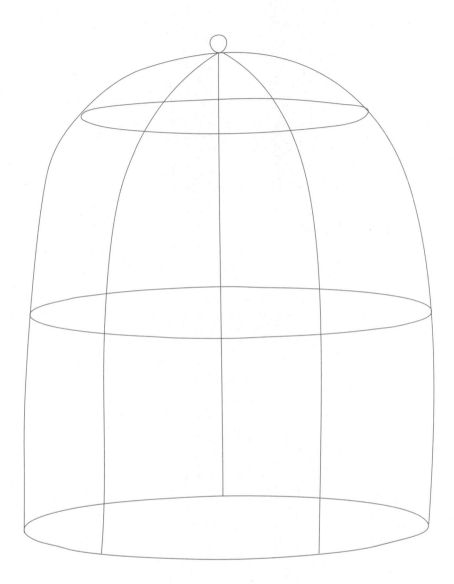

My Caged Self

Here is a cage. Inside the cage, you should draw any aspect of your self – a suppressed desire, a buried ambition – that you've always kept hidden from the outside world but secretly wish you could set free.

Russian Dolls

Here is a set of Russian dolls. They represent different layers of your personality.
The largest is the one you show to strangers; the second largest is the one you show to
your friends and colleagues; the second smallest is the one you show only to your closest
friend or partner; the very smallest is known only to yourself.

Decorate each doll, giving it an expression, costume and other symbols that embody
that particular side of your personality.

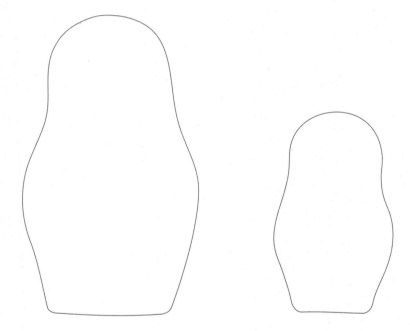

My Inner Critic

The vast majority of us have an 'inner critic' – a negative internal voice that admonishes us for our supposed failings (laziness, awkwardness, cowardice).

Draw your inner critic. Give it a name and a face – ones as ugly as the pronouncements it makes. This will help you to recognise them whenever they rear their head. Of course, the inner critic might be someone you know well, even a parental figure, which may be sobering but important to recognise.

My Inner Idiot

Typically, we spend a lot of time maintaining a particular image of ourselves – one where we appear to be a respectable, serious, dignified individual. In reality, we know we are very far from this image; most of the time, we feel (and act) more like idiots. And that's okay; we are, after all, loveable idiots.

With kindness and compassion towards yourself, draw a caricature of your inner idiot – the version of yourself that trips on the stairs, spills drinks down your front, and generally bumbles through life but is nonetheless worthy of tenderness and a good-natured smile.

Maturity Milestones

This line represents your emotional growth, from the moment you were born to the present day. Along this line, plot any significant emotional milestones that helped you become the person you are today. Examples might include the loss of a parent, breaking up with a toxic partner, or overcoming a professional setback or addiction. You can represent these milestones using either words or images.

My Safe Space

Draw yourself a 'safe space' – a place where you would feel calm, secure and protected from the difficulties of the wider world. It might be an actual place, or one that exists in your imagination. Try to make it look as safe and inviting as possible.

My Epitaph

As we get older, we tend to grow increasingly mindful of our reputation, wondering how others might remember us after we're gone.

On the headstone above, write and design your epitaph: one that sums you up in the nicest possible way, and captures how you would like to be remembered after your death.

3   Mood

We can often sense the 'mood' of an artwork. A Turner landscape may be calm; a Klimt artwork, joyous. The paintings of Georges Seurat are nostalgic and wistful, whereas those of Francis Bacon are anxious and disturbed.

In many cases, such moods reflect the current mental state or temperament of the artist themselves. In 1900, the then 19-year-old Pablo Picasso moved to Paris, where he spent several difficult years living in relative poverty, and having little success with his art. This became his 'blue' period, where all his paintings were done in a monochromatic blue/green hue, later renowned for their profoundly sober, melancholy mood. They are a testament to the way our emotions reflect our reality, creating the prism through which we interpret our thoughts and perceptions. In a sense, we are always seeing the world – and ourselves – through mood-tinted glasses.

In the following exercises, you'll be asked to create drawings that reflect particular moods. In each case, you might wish to wait until you are currently experiencing this mood before attempting the exercise – or, alternatively, try to conjure it through the act of drawing. The intent is to help you to acknowledge the role an emotion plays in your life and gain a little liberation from it.

Pathetic Fallacy

Draw your current emotional state as though it were a band of weather over a landscape. Is it sunny or cloudy? Calm or turbulent? Might there be rain or even lightning?

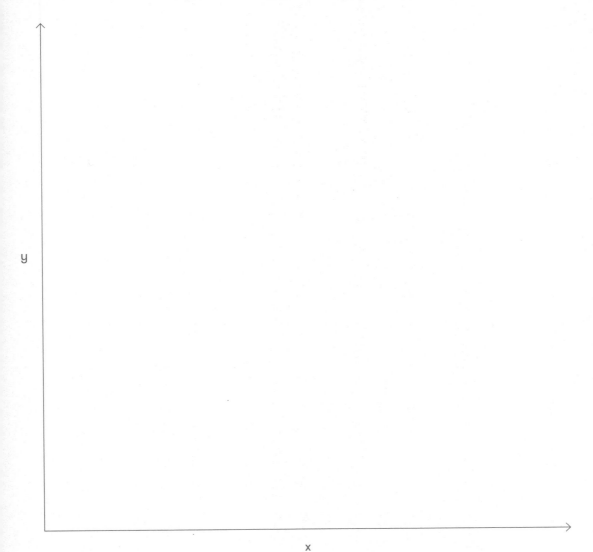

Mood Mountain Range

Over the course of a day, plot a graph that shows your mood – a single line that rises when you're in a positive mood and falls when you're in a negative one. It will probably resemble a mountain range. What caused the peaks, and what the valleys? Write down or draw these causes above or below each.

Joy

Joy tends to express itself in movement. When we feel joyful, we want to move – leaping, dancing, twirling.

Allow your pen or pencil to move joyfully. Don't worry about drawing anything in particular; simply allow your hand to leap, dance or twirl across the page.

Anger

Draw your anger as a raging monster. How big is it? What colour is it? Does it have teeth? What might its ire be directed against?

Melancholy

Melancholy is a species of sadness that arises from an acknowledgement of life's inherent difficulty. Human suffering is inevitable: all of us must cope with disappointment and pain.

Draw some of the things that conjure a feeling of melancholy. It might be a dilapidated building or a stray animal, a hospital bed or a child's grave.

Envy

We're often taught that envy is a bad emotion that no one normal should feel. In reality, it's impossible not to envy things others have, and it's best to own up maturely to the problem, perhaps as a prelude to refocusing our ambitions, or mourning our incapacities.

Here is a series of trophies. Each one represents something you envy in other people. Make them look desirable, decorating them with ornate details and jewels, and give them labels such as 'PROFESSIONAL SUCCESS' or 'A COSY RELATIONSHIP'.

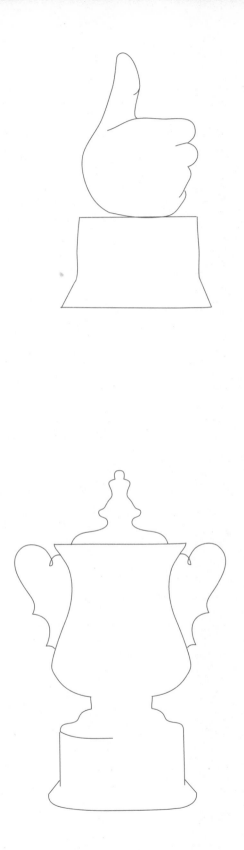

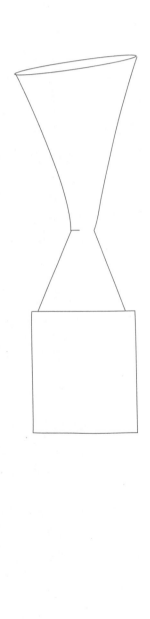

Hatred

Spend two to five minutes drawing or writing down anything and everything you hate. Don't self-censor: this is a private, cathartic act for you to express the powerful emotions you often keep suppressed.

Depression

Draw what depression feels like.

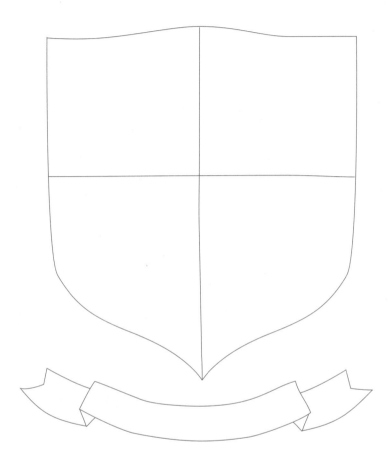

Emotional Coat of Arms

Draw an emotional coat of arms. In each of the four quarters of the shield, draw a symbol that embodies a particular emotion – the ones you experience most often, and that colour your approach to life and view of the world.

Below it, write your emotional motto: a statement summarising how the sum of these four emotions defines you as a person.

Emotional Planner

Write down three or more emotions you would like more of in your life, such as excitement, passion, enchantment, serenity, pride or silliness. Make each word stand out, and decorate them with images of things that might help you spark this emotion. Use this as a guide to planning your future: a blueprint for incorporating more emotional intensity into your life.

4   Memory

In a sense, every picture is a memory – the likeness of a time, place, or person, or a feeling now lost or changed forever. We draw to help preserve or summon the past. Although few artists draw entirely from memory, many are drawn to subjects that in some way embody their childhood and youth: boyhood landscapes, or girlhood figures.

In certain ways, art is a more suitable medium for capturing our pasts than writing. Many of our memories – particularly our earliest – are primarily visual, or sensory. What we may struggle to capture or convey through language may be more suited to embodiment in shapes, lines and symbols. The act of drawing from memory, delving into the recesses of our minds, can dredge up details and impressions we may not have expected.

In the following exercises, you'll be creating drawings inspired by memories. You won't necessarily be asked to create an image of the past (in the matter of a photograph, say) but rather to focus more on evoking the sensual character of a particular time; not a record of how it looked, but a representation of how it felt, and continues to feel to this day.

My Sketchy First Memory

Draw your earliest memory. It is likely to be a hazy, sensory memory, not an event or an incident, but a recollection of a particular image (a patterned wallpaper; your mother's face) or sensation.

Don't add detail where none exists: capture the sketchy nature of your memory.

My Bedroom

Draw your childhood bedroom from memory. Try to include all the details you remember: perhaps the pattern of the bedspread, or the shape of the bedside lamp, or the favourite toy you kept by your pillow.

My Parents

Take what you know about your parents when they were young, before they had you. Consider them with compassion and curiosity. Then try to draw them. Beside the picture, jot down what you imagine to have been their vulnerabilities and their strengths. Enjoy making a properly rounded portrait, psychologically speaking.

Imaginary Friend

As children, many of us had imaginary friends – an invented, benevolent companion we conjured to alleviate our loneliness, act as our confessor, and soothe us in difficult moments.

If you had one, draw your imaginary friend. Were they a human, or an animal, or maybe an invented creature? Did they wear a particular outfit?

If you didn't have one, draw the person, animal or object that played a nurturing role in your life – someone you could confide and place absolute trust in, and who you regularly went to for comfort.

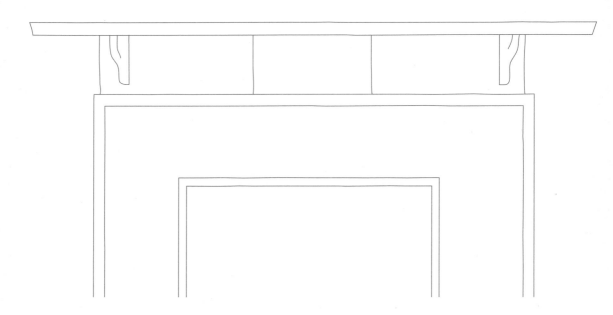

Lost and Found

Draw a formerly treasured possession you have now lost – perhaps a favourite toy, or a family heirloom. Alternatively, it might be a psychological quality (hope, innocence or trust). Preserve in a portrait what has been 'lost to the world'.

First Love

On this poster, draw the first person that you remember romantically (or sexually) desiring, as if they were hung on the wall of your bedroom as a teenager. As you draw, try to focus your mind on what it was that sparked your interest, and how this might have shaped your present tastes and choices in love.

My Happiest Memory

Draw your happiest memory. Try to capture not only the objective reality of the situation, but how it made you feel. You may wish to include abstract elements – shapes, squiggles, colours, etc.

My Most Painful Memory

Draw your most painful memory: a moment that marked you forever, the pain of which can still be felt today. Try to capture the feelings it conjured as well as the real-life details.

Old Wounds

Cover this page with scars of various sizes, from tiny nicks to gaping gashes. Each one should correspond to a painful episode in your past, which you might write down beside it. Their size and severity should correspond to the pain and significance of the hurt they have caused you. Reflect on how many scars you have sustained and on how, despite them, you have managed to persevere.

Remember This...

Despite the vastness of our memory, most of what we experience – incidents, days, weeks, perhaps even whole years of our lives – will eventually be lost.

Pick a recent memory that you wish to hold onto. It need not be anything significant – just a small moment of pride or pleasure that would otherwise be lost to time. Preserve it here for posterity.

5 Love

The relationship between art and love is very deep.
The canon is filled with famous portraits of loving
couples (Van Eyck's *Arnolfini Portrait*; Klimt's
The Kiss), beloved partners or mistresses (Goya's
Duchess; Rossetti's *Proserpine*) or embodiments of
love itself (Botticelli's *The Birth of Venus*).

Portraiture can be seen as an act of love in that it necessitates paying prolonged and intense attention to a subject, capturing its every detail in order to create an object of beauty. It is akin to the attention paid by lovers to the objects of their affection (which goes some way to explain the long history of artists having affairs with their muses).

In the following exercises, you'll be exploring your relationships and romantic history through drawing. A number of them ask you to reflect on your relationship with your current partner (skip this if you are single), and several call for your partner to participate in the exercise with you. The act of creating a drawing together – whether as artist and subject, or artists both – can be profoundly intimate, reawakening us to all that is valuable in the other, and helping to heal rifts and misunderstandings.

Relationships Map

Plot a map of your past relationships. Place yourself in the centre and draw lines that reach out to anyone and everyone you have been connected to romantically: teenage crushes, first boyfriends or girlfriends, ex-husbands and wives.

Along these lines, write down any important information that this relationship has taught you: what you learnt; what you might regret; what was nice (and not so nice) about them.

If you run out of space, don't worry – you've simply demonstrated the sheer span of your affection.

Secret Love Notes

On this page, you'll find four blank love notes. They are addressed to people in your past or present who you might have had some feeling for but never plucked up the courage to confess.

On each, write a brief, secret love note that contains what you wished you could have said to them at the time, or perhaps still wish to now. Decorate them with symbols of your affection.

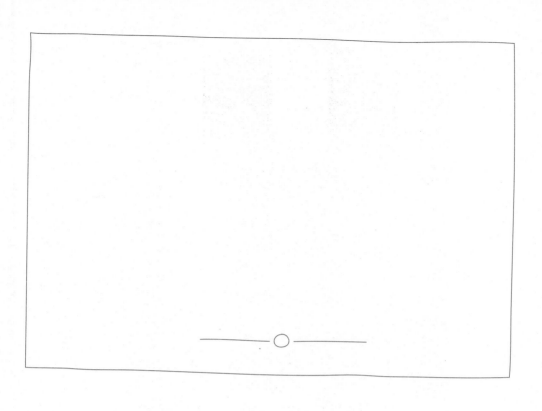

Private Screams

In relationships, we tend to hold back from saying certain things that might disturb or upset our partners – things that, at times, we wish we could scream.

If you have such a scream, give voice to it here. Spell it out in the largest possible letters.

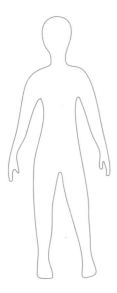

What Separates Us?

On either side of this page, you'll find two figures. They represent you and your partner.

In between, draw anything and everything that separates you – any people, objects, proclivities or other issues that come between you and make love more difficult than it might otherwise be.

Consider discussing these with your partner with an eye to finding a way through (or beyond) them.

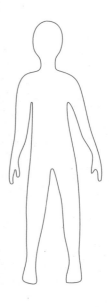

The Story of Us

Draw the moment when you first met your current partner. You might draw a static scene, or perhaps a comic strip that details the narrative of your meeting. Consider using thought or speech bubbles to re-capture what you were thinking and feeling.

You might ask your partner to complete the same exercise, then compare your various memories of your earliest encounter.

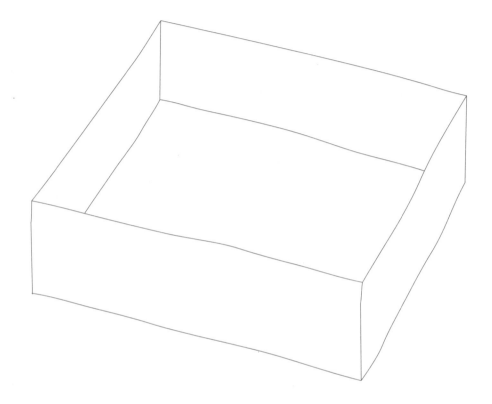

Our Box of Secrets

Every couple has shared secrets – pet names, in-jokes or private memories that they keep hidden from all others, reserved only for themselves. Such secrets bind us together: they form the basis of a shared conspiracy against the world.

Above, you'll find an open box. Fill it with your shared secrets. Write or draw them to be as small as possible.

My Beloved's Hand

Take your partner's hand and try to draw it very carefully. Pay attention to it, as if for the first time. Capture the shape of the nails, the wrinkles on the knuckles, the hairs, the bones, the pores...

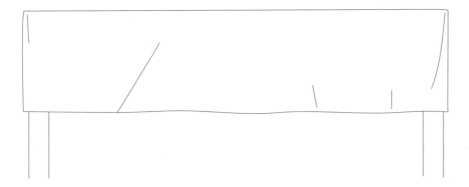

At the Altar

Design and draw an altar to your loved one. Populate it with the symbols, objects and decorations you might place there to commemorate and honour them.

Wish You Were Here

It is a truism of love that time spent apart helps us remember everything we appreciate about our partner.

Design and draw the postcard (both front and back) you might send to a loved one were you separated by a vast distance. Write the message you might send, filling it with everything that you miss about them in their absence.

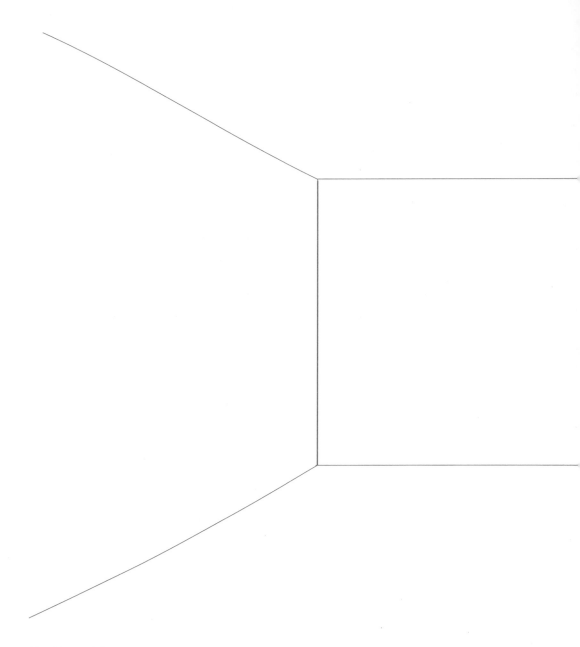

Happily Ever After

In the room above, imagine a domestic scene occurring near the end of your life – one in which you are perfectly settled and fulfilled with your partner or loved one. Draw it, imagining the setting you are in, and how you might pass a contented afternoon together.

Use this as a guide to planning your future together.

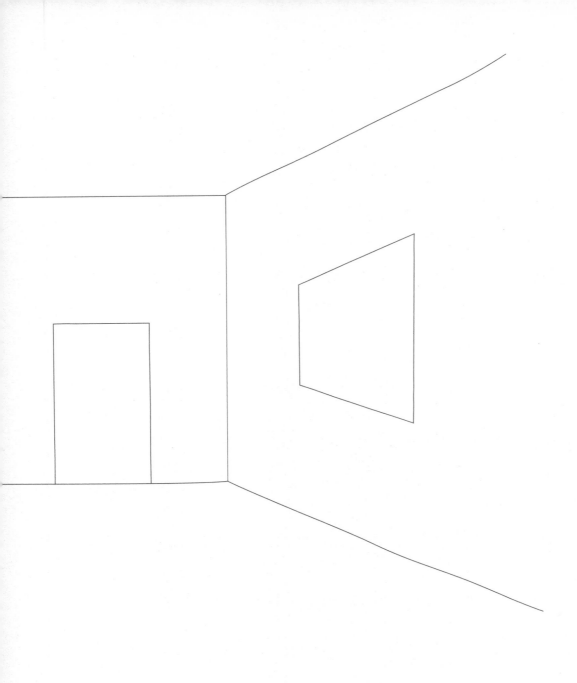

6   Calm

Art is never merely entertainment. Those of us who regularly visit galleries and exhibitions are probably acquainted with the calming quality that many works of art exert upon their viewers, like Claude Monet's *Poppies*, or Caspar David Friedrich's *Rocky Reef on the Sea Shore*. They are not merely nice to look at; they quiet our minds and soothe our souls.

It is not only the art itself, but the act of its creation that can be soothing. As in many forms of meditation, drawing can distract us from our worries and racing thoughts by refocusing our attention on a physical action. Whether we're working on an intricate portrait or merely hatching a square or joining the dots, the act itself is a tonic against panic and anxiety. The effect may be magnified if that same anxiety is the subject of the art itself. It allows us to face up to our troubles by setting them down on paper, where we can see and process them more clearly.

In the following exercises, you'll be focusing on the calming qualities of art, both in its meditative and therapeutic embodiments. In some, you'll be taking your mind off your anxieties through drawing. In others, you'll be facing those anxieties directly as a means of exorcising them: depicting them in art, so that you might better process them in thought.

The Very Worst Thing

When we're anxious, we tend to fixate on a speculative worst-case scenario, no matter how unlikely it may be. In psychology, this is known as 'catastrophising'.

Focusing on a present anxiety, draw the very worst thing you can imagine happening. This is both to help you confront your fear head-on, but also to help you place it in perspective. Perhaps reflect on how unlikely it is that it will come about, and how, even if it did, you would be able to survive.

Secret Scribbles

Whenever you next feel anxious, turn to this page and spend 30 seconds scribbling.
Wear away your panic through the nib of your pen or pencil.

Afterwards, consider turning these scribbles into a drawing in the manner of Donald
Winnicott's Scribble Game*. Your drawings should in some way embody the frustration
you were feeling; they might be spiky little gremlins of worry, or a dark, foreboding cloud.
[*See the section on Play, page 12]

The Wisdom of Cows

If there is one animal that best embodies a serene, untroubled mindset, it is surely the cow.

Draw a cow. Place it in a suitably bucolic setting (a lush, peaceful hillside or paddock) and give it an utterly relaxed expression.

Audible Illustrations

Find somewhere quiet to sit. Then, focus very carefully on all the different sounds you can hear. Birdsong, distant traffic, your own heartbeat...

As you focus on each sound, begin drawing on the paper – lines, shapes and symbols that somehow correspond to the sounds you can hear. Loud sounds might be jagged lines; softer ones, smooth lines.

Keep going until you have illustrated each of the individual sounds you can hear.

Serenity: An Exhibition

Imagine you are visiting a much-lauded new art exhibition called 'Serenity' – a collection of some of the most calming artworks in the world.

Look at the three blank frames in front of you. Imagine the exceptionally calm pictures they might contain. They shouldn't be busy or intricate – the most calming works are often the most simple.

Now, draw them in their frames.

Spirals

Anxiety tends to manifest as obsessive, self-flagellating trains of thought. If you're late for a meeting, you might start to fixate on how incompetent you are; that your boss knows you're a fraud; that you're a terrible human being, and deserve to be disgraced. This is known as spiralling.

Draw a large, wide spiral in the centre of the page. In between the lines of the spiral, write down some of the thoughts that circle your mind whenever you are very anxious. Observe how unfairly your thoughts move towards total disaster; try to temper your over-vigilant mind.

3 a.m. Doodles

Perhaps the most common side effect of anxiety is insomnia. The worries and troubling thoughts we've tried to ignore during the day tend to plague us when we're lying quietly in bed, keeping sleep at bay.

This page is reserved for doodling on between the hours of 1 a.m. and 5 a.m. Doing so will not only help distract you (and bring on sleep), but also yield some deeply imaginative artwork – between these hours, our unconscious mind asserts itself in all its brilliant weirdness.

Geometry

When our minds are consumed by chaos – racing thoughts; vague fears – we crave order and simplicity.

Practise drawing some perfectly geometrical 3D objects: cubes, cones, spheres, pyramids, and so on. Consider the effect these embodiments of mathematical harmony have on your turbulent mind.

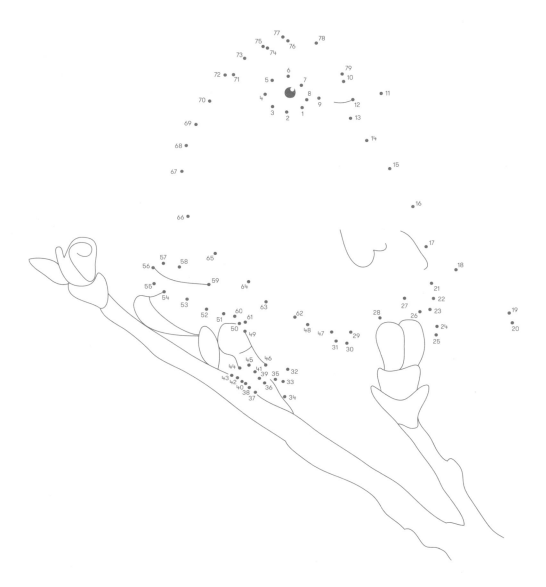

Join the Dots

Alongside colouring in, joining the dots can feel uniquely soothing. Freedom means uncertainty, anxiety; now and then, it is relaxing to surrender control and follow an established pattern.

When you next feel anxious, complete this drawing above by joining the dots in the order specified.

How to Self-Soothe

Draw some of the things that you yourself find soothing. It might be a hot bath or a favourite old blanket; a dish of comfort food or an embrace from a loved one. When anxious, you can turn to this page for a simple visual guide to some methods of self-soothing.

7 Perspective

When we are taught to draw, one of the first things we learn about is perspective: where we should place the vanishing point; how to angle the orthogonal lines; whether our perspective is one-point, two-point, or multiple. Here, the concept is wholly technical, meant to convey a sense of consistent reality to our drawing.

But there are other, more abstract ways of thinking about perspective in drawing – in particular, how it relates to our own perspective on the world around and within us. A picture of a vast landscape might cause us to reflect on our own insignificance, helping us recognise how small and inconsequential we (and our problems) are in the grander scheme of life. A close-up portrait, meanwhile, can do the opposite, building a sense of intimate connection with the particular subject, emphasising how closely our collective fates are bound.

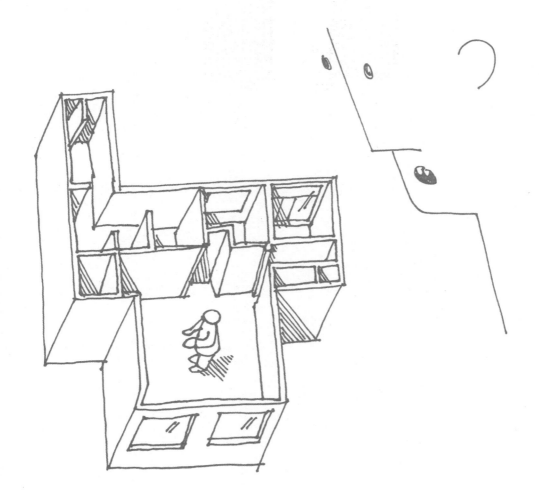

In the following exercises, you'll be adopting different perspectives: on yourself, your problems, and the world at large. You'll recognise that life can be seen from multiple vantages, and that each can help us find perspective and consolation for whatever we are going through.

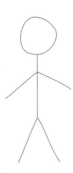

Thought Bubbles

Here is a range of stick figures. They are anonymous and interchangeable – much like the many hundreds of people you see every day.

Give each one a thought bubble. Imagine what might be currently preoccupying them: sex, money, a recipe for vegan chilli. As you draw, think about how every person you pass is never merely a background figure, but an entire, endless consciousness, with all the complexity you recognise in your own self.

A Million Tiny Problems

Can you find the tiny dot somewhere on this page? Imagine it represents the problem you're currently facing – a difficult relationship, an unpaid bill.

Fill the rest of this page with as many dots as you can draw. Imagine each dot represents another person's problem: an unfaithful partner, an impending performance review.

As you draw, think about how this might change your perspective on the scale of your present concerns.

Ludolf Bakhuysen, *Warships in a Heavy Storm*, 1695

Perseverance

In Dutch Golden Age art, there is a tradition of painting ships being tossed about in heavy seas. These paintings served a symbolic function, reminding us of our capacity to endure through trials, setbacks and turbulent times.

Draw your own such picture, using the height and ferocity of the waves to represent the challenges you face, and the size and position of the ship to represent your capacity to traverse them. You might write down words or phrases and fix them to particular waves, to remind yourself of what you are up against.

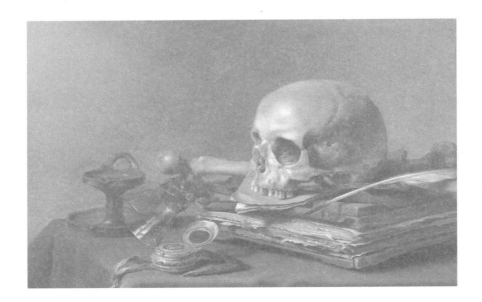

Pieter Claesz, *Vanitas Still Life*, 1630

Vanitas

Vanitas was a style of art popular in early modern Europe: still lifes of objects that symbolised transience, like hourglasses, rotting fruit and skulls. They were meant to act as a reminder that life is short, time is limited, and that we squander both at our peril.

Draw your own vanitas. You can use real-life objects as reference, or simply use your imagination. Fill the scene with images that remind you that your time on Earth is ever-shortening, and that death is around the corner.

Sublime View

The Romantics invented (or discovered) the notion of the sublime: a powerful feeling of awe that comes from contemplating an unfathomable vastness, such as when we look up at an immense mountain, or down into the depths of the ocean. They theorised that it arose from a sudden understanding of our own ultimate insignificance.

Draw a sublime view, looking up at a mountain, or down into a valley, or a view of the Earth from space. As you draw, focus on a sense of your own smallness.

Something Old

Draw something that is older than yourself. It might be a family heirloom or an old building; a historical landmark or an ageing tree. Try to find the oldest thing you can find to draw from life.

Pay particular attention to any markers of its age – cracks, accumulated dirt, moss and lichen, or other signs of wear and tear.

Perhaps reflect on how this object has, despite these markers, managed to endure, and will continue to do so into the future.

Prehistoric Art

The earliest examples of artistic expression are cave paintings. The oldest known cave painting, discovered in Spain, is more than 64,000 years old. Such paintings are a testament to humanity's long and enduring relationship with art and creativity.

Draw your own cave painting. Look up some examples and draw some simple sketches in the style of prehistoric art – perhaps of the modern objects that define your life, like computers or phones. Imagine how the present moment would look from the perspective of the far, far future.

Staring Out the Window

Spend 10 to 15 minutes drawing the view through your bedroom window. Try to include as much detail as you can, and incorporate some of the people, animals or vehicles that happen to pass by.

Antipodean View

Draw in landscape a view from the opposite side of the world of where you are currently residing.

You can use the internet to work out the most distant point from where you are now (through a site like antipodesmap.com), then use an online map to find a photograph of that place. If it happens to be in the ocean, find the nearest land or habitation to that point and draw a view from there instead.

How different does the landscape look at its furthest point away from you? Or, how similar?

A Home Within a Home

Looking around your flat, house or garden, try to find any examples of animal habitation. It might be a spider's web or a bird's nest, a mouse hole or a beehive. You should be able to find at least one.

Draw any you can find, reflecting, as you do so, how a different species of life exists in the backdrop of your own.

8   Re-enchantment

To draw is to become enchanted – if only briefly – with a subject. The act both demands and induces a fascination with whatever we are drawing. This is one reason why we draw more as children than we do as adults. As children, the world seems endlessly new and vital. As adults, it has become familiar, commonplace and, therefore, less obviously a source of enchantment.

By compelling ourselves to draw, we can become re-enchanted with existence. Our lives are so busy, our time so short, that we rarely take the time to pay attention to all that is beautiful, pleasurable and valuable in the world around us: autumn leaves, starry skies, or even just the view from our bedroom window. Drawing forces us to look again – to look more closely, raptly, and with a sense of wonder and gratitude for the miracle of life. Through drawing, we learn to appreciate this miracle anew – to see it as a child or newborn does, with fresh and grateful eyes.

In the following exercises, you'll be learning to appreciate life itself – to feel gratitude for the present and hope for the future. You won't necessarily be drawing anything grand or impressive, but rather the small, unheralded pleasures that make life worth living. You'll be paying them the highest compliment a person can offer: to capture, preserve and celebrate them through art.

John Ruskin, *Cluster of Oak Leaves*, 1856

Seeing Leaves

The artist and critic John Ruskin (1819–1900) was the foremost authority on art of the Victorian age. In his 1857 book *The Elements of Drawing*, he emphasised the role of art as appreciation – that drawing a given subject requires a recognition of its subtlety and beauty. He advised all aspiring artists to begin by learning how to draw a leaf.

Find a leaf. Spend five to ten minutes sketching it in as much detail as possible. Try to capture its shape, its texture, the structure of its veins. As you do so, reflect on the intricacy and beauty of the natural world.

Dream House

Draw your dream house. It might be small and cosy, or vast and palatial; situated in green countryside, or by a spotless beach; designed to look ultra-modern, or perfectly classical.

Focus on your vision. If pressed, how might you go about making it a reality?

Utopia

Draw the skyline of a future utopian city. What types of buildings are there? What sort of businesses occupy these buildings? What form of transport are people using? How does this city improve upon those of the past?

Favourite View

Many of us have a favourite view – from a hilltop, park bench, or high window – that brings us a sense of profound contentment.

When you next have a spare afternoon, go there and sketch the landscape. Alternately, if this is not possible, sketch it from memory.

Everyday Pleasures

We tend to place our hopes for happiness in far-off, hard-to-obtain pleasures – like luxury items, or expensive holidays – forgetting that there are many everyday pleasures that, in a small but significant way, make our lives worth living.

Draw a sample of some simple everyday pleasures you enjoy; ones that are easy to find and available for almost nothing, but that nonetheless bring brightness into your day. Perhaps a hot cup of tea, or a misty morning; a kind gesture from a partner, or the face of a pet or child.

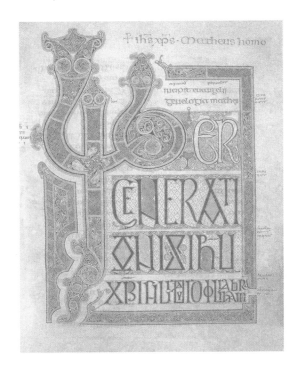

An illustrated page from the Lindisfarne Gospels.

Illuminated Quotation

'Illumination' is a term that describes decorating a piece of text with beautiful imagery. It was practised by medieval scribes, who would decorate biblical verses or other writing with ornate lettering and imagery – the Lindisfarne Gospels are a characteristic example.

Choose a favourite quotation from a book, poem or thinker that means something to you. 'Illuminate' it with decorative lettering and symbols to bring it to life. You might wish to place your artwork somewhere prominent in your home as a constant (and beautiful) reminder of a truth you wish to remember.

Certificate of Achievement

When we were young, it is likely we were presented with a certificate commemorating an achievement we could take pride in, like passing a music exam or learning how to swim. Now we are old, we probably don't get such certificates – which is a great shame, for there is much in our lives we can still take pride in.

Design yourself a certificate commemorating something you have achieved in the emotional sphere – like being an adequate parent, or managing to find a job you can feel proud of, or, simply and as importantly, for making it through to the end of another day (that's achievement enough). Make it look as special as possible.

Learning from the Masters

If you can, go to an art gallery; if not, look online. Find a painting that you enjoy, preferably a large one, and one that speaks to you in some way.

Focus on a small detail of that artwork, one that doesn't seem too difficult to reproduce: the hand of a figure, or a face in the crowd. Spend 10 to 15 minutes creating a sketch of that detail. Doing so will force you to look at (and appreciate) the art in much greater detail than you would ordinarily.

Pioneering Portrait

Given how many paintings there are in the world, we might assume that there is little in our life that hasn't found its way into a work of art. On the contrary, there is much that has rarely, or ever, received attention from artists. For example: can you remember seeing a portrait of a shoelace? An internet modem? A pothole? An Allen key?

Find an ordinary, unheralded object that you can't remember seeing in a painting before. Draw it, trying to focus on what, from a certain angle, might make it beautiful.

Constellations

The next time there is a clear sky at night, go outside and plot a map of the stars. Don't worry too much about accuracy, just roughly plot the position of every star you can see with a dot, star or circle.

Next, design your own constellations by drawing lines between the dots to create objects or figures. These constellations should represent significant sources of meaning in your life – perhaps an object that symbolises your craft, or a figure that stands in for someone particularly special to you. Give each constellation a name.

The School of Life is a global organisation helping people lead more fulfilled lives. It is a resource for helping us understand ourselves, for improving our relationships, our careers and our social lives – as well as for helping us find calm and get more out of our leisure hours. We do this through films, workshops, books, gifts and community. You can find us online, in stores and in welcoming spaces around the globe.

THESCHOOLOFLIFE.COM